Habits of a Productive Businessman

How to Get Things Done Fast and With Minimum Costs

By: Ruth Walker

9781635012873

I0510800

PUBLISHERS NOTES

Disclaimer – Speedy Publishing LLC

Speedy Publishing LLC

40 E Main Street, Newark, Delaware, 19711

Contact Us: 1-888-248-4521

Website: http://www.speedypublishing.co

REPRINTED Paperback Edition: 9781635012873:

Manufactured in the United States of America

DEDICATION

To my mother, Dolores. You gave me the life any girl would die for. You are my strength and my inspiration. I will always be your little girl.

TABLE OF CONTENTS

Chapter 1- Do Little, Gain More: Everybody's Dream Come True 5

Chapter 2- Position Yourself As Someone Who Can 13

Chapter 3- How do You Reduce Distractions? 22

Chapter 4- What's Keeping You From Being Productive? 32

Chapter 5- How to be More Productive? 38

Chapter 6- Of Employees, Coworkers and Supplies 46

About The Author 51

CHAPTER 1- DO LITTLE, GAIN MORE: EVERYBODY'S DREAM COME TRUE

Productivity is generally measured by the resulting outcome produced and if this outcome is acceptable then the productivity percentage is deemed acceptable too, therefore understanding the elements that are required are where the answer lies.

There are several tricks that one can apply in order to be able to be more productive without the hassle or stress it is perceived to present.

The most would be to make a list of all the tasks expected of the individual and then eliminating those tasks that either don't require the individual's hand on participation or are not that urgent to start with.

This not only allows the individual to focus on only the necessary tasks but also relieves the individual from its possible distractions.

Setting daily goals with the main goal always in focus also helps in the effort to keeping things on track and in focus always. It also eliminates the tendency to waste time on processes that will not eventually positively contribute to the goal.

Identifying one's own peak times for productivity is also another important element to take advantage of. Having the energy to be productive throughout the day is not only unlikely it is also improbable; therefore there is a need to capitalize on the productivity time frame and get as much done within this frame as possible.

Being in a work conducive environment is also something that should be given due consideration as this will directly affect the producing results.

Too many distractions will take the focus of the individual away from completing the tasks according to the pre prepared schedules and thus cause the overall timeline to be disrupted. This could then cause temporary derailment from the overall work schedule towards achieving the goal.

What Does It Take for an Entrepreneur to Succeed?

Let's suppose you planned to be at your PC, working at a project, at 10 a.m. on a Monday morning, but you're not. How come? The answer may be one or more of the accompanying.

The Enemies

• Woke up late.

- Scrapped with your lover last night, and continue reliving the quarrel in your brain.

- Are too sapped – the coffee hasn't set in yet.

- Are overly hyper – drank too much coffee and can't sit motionless.

- Are disquieted by the weather – it's amazing out and you'd love to take a walk or bike ride.

- Are disquieted by the weather – it's atrocious and depressing.

- Got a telephone call (or e-mail or instant message) from a friend, who's depressed (though not in crisis) and asked to talk.

- Got a telephone call from a friend (or e-mail or instant message) that's happy and wished to share great news.

- Are reading the paper – every last word of it.

- Are net surfing or net shopping.

- Are playing Solitaire.

- Simply realized that it's highly crucial to work on another project.

- Or, if you work in a home office:

- Switched on the television set for "a minute" and saw that one of your favorite actors was being interviewed, so you decide to view the interview.

- Simply realized that the laundry urgently needs to get done!

These are common things that may throw you off your course. It's only a partial list; naturally, you may likely add many other entries to it. There are likely 100s of potential "bumps" that may knock you off your course.

One crucial thing to point out is that, while a few of these bumps appear "good" or "worthwhile" (like commiserating with your unhappy acquaintance or doing the laundry), and some seem "foul" or "frivolous" (like playing Solitaire), they're all equally unacceptable from the viewpoint of beating your procrastination habit.

You'll need to learn to resist the urge to get absorbed into activities not on your schedule, regardless how crucial or virtuous they appear at the moment. The one exception, naturally, is emergencies, by which I mean actions that can't be put off without significant harm to yourself or other people. However even with an emergency, after you've handled it, ask yourself whether it may have been prevented by finer planning, or whether somebody else could have handled it. If you've got a challenging goal, it's really crucial to learn to minimize the number of preventable emergencies in your life, and to learn to delegate as much as conceivable.

Procrastinators are frequently adept at rationalizing their diversions. Obviously, if somebody is ill or otherwise incapacitated, we ought to help them, but to what degree? It's not always clear, and a lot of procrastinators misjudge, sacrificing too much of their own time to assist other people, even when those other people aren't particularly needy or when somebody else is available to help. This issue may be hard to identify, much less solve, as the (deservedly) good feeling one gets from assisting frequently offsets the guilt that the procrastination commonly spawns.

The net entrepreneur can't enjoy any of their business success if they're dropping off customers, running out of time - not being able to bill their customers for that time, or unable to complete their projects.

Being able to successfully handle projects is among the key indicators of a home business enterpriser who manages their time well. Do they manage by crises or by intent? Is it part of their goal to go either slowly or quickly in project management, aiming toward a wanted result?

The affect that this may have on the work from home entrepreneur impacts any potential succeeding business and may likewise taint their net reputation. All of this is tied into suitable and effective time management! Is there an answer for this hurdle?

What is the Ultimate Secret to Business Success?

Managing time effectively is maybe the number 1 goal of most every work at home enterpriser on their quest for success. Without having effective time management, their net businesses suffer despairingly.

Making originative utilization of their time is the goal of most every work at home enterpriser who wishes to be successful in their home businesses. Effective time management will let the work at home entrepreneur be able to achieve more with their time and have fulfilled buyers and a well-fixed business.

Effective time management calls for a determined range of skills, strategies and tools and helps the net entrepreneur use them in order to achieve particular tasks, projects and goals. Without the strategic utilization of their time, they're basically wasting their time and unable to complete crucial business goals.

Habits of a Productive Businessman

It's really crucial for the net entrepreneur to effectively manage time in their home business for a lot of reasons:

• They may complete projects in a timely manner

If they're able to be effective in finishing projects, they may take on more work; more employees and better fulfill their client loads by efficiently meeting deadlines.

• They're better able to create quality work

More quality work results when there's more time and more attention to particulars given to the work. Quality work may only be a result of careful tending and thoroughness to detail.

• They may secure more work as they're able to meet deadlines

As a work at home enterpriser, meeting deadlines for your customers is like guaranteed work! Virtually everything on the Net is time-sensitive so when you're able to meet deadlines, you show that you're responsible and committed to the task at hand.

• R.O.I.

There's a substantial return on investment with attention to particulars in the home business of the entrepreneur once they may effectively handle their time. If they may get more done in the course of a span of time, they lessen the amount of time to get the job accomplished, but are still able to make the same, if not more cash. The return on their investment (planning time) is fantastic!

• Gratification

There's an overall feeling of gratification and achievement when the online entrepreneur completes a task. The feeling of completion acts as a motivator and provides him or her creative spark they require to either approach a fresh customer or stir up more business with old customers.

These factors are commonly motivators for the work at home enterpriser to handle their time well and discover originative ways to work more efficiently. It's commonly the little details of running a business (like managing time) that help the entrepreneur make good on his business matters.

All the same, there are not always good times or simple times when all goes well with the entrepreneur who attempts to get a lot of things done in the course of their business relations. When they're responsible for each phase of their business, there's always the potential of failure or frustration for lack of planning or organizing.

What occurs when time management doesn't work well or produce the wanted results?

Are all net entrepreneurs challenged on the subject of time management?

There are times that the work from home enterpriser discovers that their systems and procedures aren't working. They discover that regardless what they do, they can't remain focused and finish the tasks or goals that they have. They discover that they're basically poorly managing their time and unable to accomplish neither small nor big goals.

Habits of a Productive Businessman
Poor time management could be the perpetrator.

CHAPTER 2- POSITION YOURSELF AS SOMEONE WHO CAN

For a large portion of society things don't come easy and there are no "free" handouts at every turn, thus the needs to be strong and adopt the "can do" attitude very early on in life.

With this positive attitude firmly in place very few obstacles can pose a problem as the individual will be able to look at it in a more positive light. Having a can do mentality takes practice and perseverance, and it is not impossible to adopt. Some of the tools to help cultivate this positive mentality are as follows:

• Always have a healthy measure of faith both in the endeavor being explored and in one's own capability. This is perhaps the most important ingredient to ensure any successful experience. This faith will see the individual through when things seem difficult and failure look possible.

- Being as knowledgeable as possible will also contribute positively to this mental go getting state of mind. When one is knowledgeable, tackling different tasks and experiences will not be daunting and have an advantage that only knowledge can provide.

- Being a go getter also means that shyness is not part of one's personality. Being shy will dampen any attempts to be open to opportunities, thus should strive to keep this particular personality trait well under control.

- Looking the part is also recommended when one is pursuing success. This does not necessarily mean dressing expensively or having expensive accessories or toys. It simply means displaying the confidence that is needed to ensure other parties are impressed enough to relax and accept one's point of view on whatever is being discussed.

- Learn how to "wow" people with your personality and knowledge without coming off boorish or pompous. This is an art that when practiced to refinement, can enable the solicitation of almost anything from anyone.

Know Your Goals and How to Organize Them

There are a lot of tried and true methods that are available for the exercise of identifying and organizing goals. Being able to have a set plan in place is the first step to ensuring success in its highest percentage possible.

Therefore understanding and then creating a plan towards the eventual successful completion of a goal is a very important and advantageous exercise to embark upon. The following are just some recommendations to this end:

Setting out the details of the goals should be the first step to seeing its completion. When there are clear indications of all the different aspects of the exercise in place the individual is better able to organize the various exercises involved in the process.

Then there are the priority lists that should be drawn up. These would require the individual to identify and prioritize the various different aspects of the whole exercise according to its importance in relation to keeping the general flow of the endeavor smooth and on track always.

Folder management is one tool that many have found very useful when embarking on a project that requires the coordination of various connective elements.

Documenting and storing any sort of data in the relevant folders will ensure the said data is easily available and accessible to a moment's notice. Confusion and delays can easily be avoided if this method is implemented and diligently practiced.

Keep a strict monitoring of all due dates is very important, as the efficient running of any endeavor depends on this. When due dates are not taken seriously there will be a lack of urgency to have tasks completed, which in turn will upset the general flow of the project.

Having a periodical check and balance list in place, is also another way to ensure the goals are met in a well-organized way. These periodical checks will help all concerned to monitor the general overall progress and address any areas that need attention immediately.

There's a Need to Break down Goals to Perform Better

Breaking down a list of items within each progressive state of the endeavor will allow all involved to work independently and collaboratively. With smaller tasks listed the entire experience will not feel so overwhelming and unmanageable. Some of the areas that should be considered to ensure optimization of both resources as well as other contributing elements are as follows:

Each goal should have many sub goals which are easier to handle and produce faster results. These may unfold through the help of several contributing parties, each taking on a smaller part of the task to speed up the completion process.

Having a calendar drawn up to display the entire list of smaller tasks that would eventually lead up to the successful completion of the main task is also encouraged.

This visual aid will give all involved a definite and clear picture of the various steps that needs to be taken and how long each step should ideally take.

Time tracking is another tool that can complement the calendar way of keeping tabs on the project exercise. Besides gauging the general time line needed for completion it can also assist the individual in future projects launched through the learning experience from previous exercises.

There are several software products in the market today that can also help to streamline efforts required within any exercise, and the use of this would be beneficial if the individual is not very experienced.

Tags and keywords are also good in assisting those involved to be able to access any given situation quickly and accurately. Having a set list of words that can be applied to the smaller list of things will speed up the process of getting information on any particular aspect of the overall project instantly. It also helps to search for information more efficiently.

Have a Timeline

Within the exercise of setting goal in various different connective sections there is also a need to address the timeline issue and provide for a suitable one. This will help to ensure all participants become aware of the time constraints and also the requirements for each section allowed.

Letting a project run without any specific timeline firmly in place is very unwise and some would even say detrimental to the success of any project, therefore the following points are listed to help overcome this negative possibility:

Identifying one's own most productive period cycles within a working day will help to optimize the amount of productive effort put into the endeavor.

This can then be coordinated with the others involved in the project, if any, as not everyone will have the same levels of productivity at the same times. The advantage of this will give those involved a chance to identify higher priority tasks to be done during these peak cycles and leaving the lesser demanding tasks to be done during the off peak cycles; thus optimizing the timeline always.

Allotting time within the timeline to concentrate on the project without any outside communication or distractions will also contribute to the eventual completion of the project within the timeline frame.

As distractions can cause a person to lose temporary focus, this consideration is important if not vital to the overall timeline being kept.

Within each task there should be a specific time frame allotted and adhered to without exceptions. Ensuring all efforts are focused on getting the particular task completed before work is stopped, will help to keep the designed target in place.

These mini milestones will also act as a good motivating factor because the accomplishments become visible every step of the exercise.

Never Procrastinate

Nearly all ambitious dreamers, for example, have to reduce the time they spend on ho-hum household chores to as close as possible to zilch, so that they may utilize the reclaimed time and energy to work at their aspiration.

All right, if you like gardening and it feeds your soul, then don't quit. But washing? Yard work? Wiping up floors? Standing in line at the market? To the extent you're able to find somebody else to do it. Send your wash out to be done, hire somebody to maintain the lawn (or get your mate or children to do it), purchase a floor mopping robot, and have your foodstuffs delivered.

If you feel peculiar doing any of that, get over it: cutting down your housework burden is an investment in yourself. Likewise, it's unrealistic to believe that you may spend your time the same way non-ambitious dreamers do and yet achieve your challenging dream.

None of this ought to be taken to mean that you desert your loved ones or friends. It simply implies you invest your time judiciously. Even though you're not cutting your parents' lawn, for example, you may still be taking them to checkup appointments: that's a much higher value activity that's likely a far better utilization of your time.

And even though you're not fixing home cooked dinners nightly, you may still do it a few times a week. And even if you're not going to be able to speak to your friend for hours daily, you may still be available to her in times of true need.

It may be scary to alter the terms of our interaction with somebody, particularly if we've been interacting with them a particular way for years. (Double particularly if we've been taught to subordinate our needs to other people, as many women particularly are.)

Individuals frequently respond badly when we tell them we can't do as much for them, or spend as much time with them, as we have been. Frequently, however, if we take the time to share our state of affairs, aspirations and needs, they're surprisingly empathic and eager to help. So don't simply tell individuals you'll be less available tell them why, and invite their support and help.

If, after you share your story, a few individuals still aren't empathic, or are actively unfriendly, that's a sorry issue to have, but a typical one. That's why successful individuals learn to say "no", and also to distance themselves from unsupportive or toxic individuals, even if they happen to be related to them.

Whatever time you choose to spend helping other people you ought to build into your weekly or monthly schedule. You ought to likewise build in time both for your own relaxation and for unintentional events and emergencies.

Many individuals think time management is about attempting to stuff as much as possible into one's schedule, but it's not; it's regarding clearing as much as conceivable off your schedule so you may work, at a comfortable, non-stressful pace, on your crucial goals.

To summarize: whatever bumps you off your course that isn't an unpreventable emergency is procrastination, regardless how crucial it might seem at the time.

Second-rate time management - - does the net entrepreneur ever believe that he has poor time management? Or, does he automatically believe that he's managing his time efficiently and effectively merely because he's a business owner?

Either way, he has to cautiously guard against wasting time or not maximizing the full utilization of the flexible time that work at home entrepreneurs have. Without a self-asserting effort, he may be doomed for incompleteness or merely business failure.

Frequently, procrastination is the primary perpetrator of poor time management, but is frequently not taken as seriously as of the perceived "creativity" in waiting. Put differently, net entrepreneurs frequently have trepidation about moving too fast on business projects or making decisions too rapidly.

As noble as this might sound, it may often have the opposite effect and cause the work from home individual to move too slowly, move too fast or do nothing at all. Good time management may

Ruth Walker

help. Failing to plan in any home business isn't different from failing to plan in any other sort of business. There must be a business model formulated, a marketing strategy followed out and a plan of action to accomplish goals for the business. This all ties with the ability to create designs handle time effectively and discover which resources would work best for the business.

Planning daily might seem like a lot of work to do but in actual truth when it becomes a habit, it gets to be second nature. Studies show that it takes an average of twenty-one times for something to get to be a habit. When something does get to be a habit, it's much simpler to maintain than if it's new or from the beginning.

Home entrepreneurs have total flexibility and convenience in their occupations. There's no one standing over them, ordering their day, telling them what to accomplish, when to accomplish it, how to accomplish it, and so forth. With all of this freedom, an undisciplined individual won't understand how to effectively manage their time or when to say no to particular projects or fresh business.

For a lot of entrepreneurs, they put off their work duties or obligations for wide-ranging reasons. Doing this may cause unbelievable tension for the entrepreneur and cause them to handle or work in a crises mode.

Working in that way may produce additional issues that may become hard to solve or manage. There are errors made, uncompleted projects, missed goals, second-rate work quality and even second-rate business results.

Chapter 3- How do You Reduce Distractions?

There are few things which block productivity as fast and as surely as distractions. When you cannot concentrate and focus properly, you cannot get things done. Even if you do accomplish something, it can feel stressful and frustrating. Whether you are on the job or at school, reducing the distractions which influence your ability to be productive will help you to get more done. There are two key points which you should keep in mind when you are planning to reduce the distractions in your environment.

The first point is what works for you and what works for someone else may be entirely different. The second point is unless you have examined your habits, you may not be one hundred percent certain about the habits that are the most effective for you. The good news is it does not require much time or effort to consider how your habits are affecting your productivity, and begin to adjust them accordingly. If you are like most people these days, multi-tasking has become a part of your everyday life and your everyday vocabulary. There may be a number of things which you need to do in one day, and you may be doing them simultaneously.

If you overdo with multi-tasking, there can be two consequences. You might not get everything done; or you might spread yourself too thin and not have satisfactory results. The same can be said about distractions. Attempting to do a job-- and to do it correctly and well-- will not net satisfactory results if distractions are allowed to get in the way. Working while listening to music, watching television, or chatting on the phone is a common practice not only limited to teens. Many adults do these things in their home offices, and even in an office which is occupied by other people. Perhaps they help your concentration-- but they can just as easily ruin your concentration, and distract you from what you are doing. Becoming more productive takes a little analyzing of your habits. You can turn off some or all of these distractions, and see if you are better able to focus on the task at hand. You may find that you can get the job done better, faster, and more effectively, without any distractions at all.

On the other hand, you may find that one of these factors actually does aid in your concentration and focus. While finding whatever works for you is easy if you work on your own, it can be a little more complicated if you work with others. You may find that coworkers who constantly use their phones, visit, or play their radios near your workspace distract you from focusing on your job. If you approach them politely, this may be all it takes to reduce the distractions so you can concentrate on your job.

Habits of a Productive Businessman
Difficult First, Easy Last

If you think about back when you were in school, you may remember teachers telling you that the best way to approach homework and other projects was to do the hardest task first. They may have also advised you to tackle the homework subject you disliked the most first, before moving on. This same approach can greatly enhance your productivity today. When you are preparing to begin a fresh day at work, try to begin putting this approach into action. Instead of beginning with a task you enjoy, or one which comes easily to you, start with one you dislike, or one which you feel will be quite difficult. At the end of the day, you may be pleasantly surprised with how much you have accomplished. You will also feel that the day has gone much smoother.

One reason for this is at the start of your work day you will have more energy. When you devote this energy to the hardest or most disliked tasks, you will not feel as drained or frustrated in doing them.

A second reason is if you begin with tasks you enjoy, you often find yourself looking ahead to the ones you dislike in a very negative manner. Instead of enjoying the easier tasks while you are doing them, you are dreading the ones ahead. When you do the hardest ones first, you will not only have more energy left for the rest of the day; you will also appreciate the other tasks more when you get to them. This approach will increase your productivity. When you do not look at your work day as a long, uphill battle, you will get more accomplished.

Getting the tasks you dislike out of the way first, early in the day, will generate better results with all of your tasks. Not only will you get more done, you will be much more satisfied with the outcome of each and every task. While it is only human nature to want to do what you like first, having the harder things on the horizon can slow you down and drain your energy. If you want to be more productive, and achieve the very best results in everything you do, take the advice from your school teachers and tackle the hardest jobs first. Your productivity will increase, and you will end each day with a refreshing feeling of accomplishment.

Common Practices that Affect Your Productivity

Here are a few matters to bear in mind that may drastically affect your productivity rate when it comes to your business:

• Beginning your day with no action plan

If you begin your day with no action plan, you're damned from the start! You start off late and feel overpowered from the beginning. You then spend your day in a defensive and crisis mood.

You might likewise find yourself hurriedly and arbitrarily responding to other people's issues and events and place them higher up than your own issues.

• No equilibrium

There are 7 key areas in our lives where we have to practice equilibrium in order to feel and have success:

• Wellness - how your body feels and how it reacts to external stimulants

• Loved ones - quality time and responsibilities with loved ones

• Financial - amount of fiscal burdens and revenue obligations

Habits of a Productive Businessman

• Intellectual - how exterior stimulants affect your life

• Social - how you interact with other people

• Professional - the procedures that you utilize to advance your career

• Spiritual - your relationship with the higher power and other people

Each of these areas calls for our daily time for completeness, although they might not all get equal time every day. It's not so crucial to spend significant time in every area, but it's crucial to spend a little time in every area.

In the long haul, our lives will be balanced and harmonious if we spend a sufficient amount and quality of time in every area. All the same, if we disregard any one of these areas, we may quickly sabotage our success.

For example, if we don't take care of our wellness, our loved ones and social life suffer. Likewise, if we're out of balance in our monetary resources, we can't adequately center on our professional goals, career dreams and additional crucial areas of focus.

• Cluttered up workspace

A cluttered up workspace may produce a cluttered up work brain.

Issues result when you can't find crucial business documents or locate info for your customers. These things induce mayhem, wreak bedlam and confusion, but may likewise lead to lost revenue and delayed billing.

Studies have been conducted, proving that an individual who works with a cluttered up desk spends about one to two hours a day searching for things or being distracted by them. This may add up significantly in hours squandered per week.

• Poor rest

The perpetrator of poor rest is the blame for a lot of net entrepreneurs not meeting goals or seeing results in their businesses. Not enough sleep may lead to poorly made decisions or irrational selections as they relate to crucial business functions.

Studies have evidenced that nearly 75% of net enterprisers are sleep-deprived, and that their businesses are inadvertently impacted. Being tired isn't good or productive for the work at home individual.

If the deficiency of sleep doesn't negatively impact the entrepreneur, the caliber of their sleep will. This implies that when they do get to rest, it's commonly fitful, restless sleep because of fundamental stress and other debilitating components.

Stress-filled days are hazardous to the net entrepreneur and may eventually become detrimental. The key is to acquire enough rest and proper sleep to experience less tension and become more productive.

• Not taking breaks

Taking decent breaks and frequent breaks is a big failure of the net entrepreneur. Because they're not on a routine or rigid schedule as in a corporate scene, they feel that they shouldn't have to or can't consider breaks. They might likewise feel that doing so is a waste of time. Not truthful. Taking sufficient breaks is vital to daily successes.

A lot of times, the net entrepreneur likewise neglects to take sufficient breaks as they feel as though they may produce better results.

They feel that if they work straight through, that they may get more accomplished and be more productive. This doesn't produce more results or even better work time.

If the body is exhausted, reaction and creativity are gravely hampered and may cause the quality of the entrepreneur's work to suffer.

Many procrastinators tell themselves stuff like: "I'm lazy. I'm undisciplined. I'm a failure. I'm hopeless. I've got no self-control. I'll never win at anything."

Many creative persons, activists, and other ambitious dreamers take the self-abuse a step farther, framing their procrastination as a moral defect: "I'm a sellout, unattached, shallow".

A lot of procrastinators lead a double life, acting happy and productive while truly feeling hemmed in. Their boasts about their big workloads, power to work under pressure, and steady need to pull all-nighters are frequently just a cover for shame and despair; and frequently, when matters get really hot when they're about to miss a serious deadline, thereby showing their real, "shameful" nature they cut and run, deserting a project, class, job, relationship or other commitment."

Frequently, procrastinators become depressed almost as soon as they wake as they recognize they're destined to procrastinate that day. Procrastination may also feel really confusing.

At bedtime, you retrospect on the day and can't figure out where your time went. You remember reading the headlines, drinking a cup of java with your officemates, watching some TV, and surfing the net, but those random activities couldn't possibly have filled the whole day, could they? But, naturally, they did. Procrastination is, "the thief of time". To a procrastinator, it truly does feel as if his or her time were somehow stolen.

If a procrastination issue is severe enough, and lasts long enough, it's often called a "block", as in "writer's block". Anybody may be blocked, and many individuals, maybe most, are. Occasionally, blocks last for weeks or months, but oftentimes, tragically, they last for years, decades or even entire life spans. Being blocked is among the riskiest feelings in the world; it drives some individuals to absolute desperation.

But wait there's no need to feel ashamed or desperate! When someone confesses to a procrastination issue, I congratulate her. Yes, congratulate.

Here's how come: Procrastination is an affliction of ambitious individuals. If you don't trust me, do a net search on procrastination: you'll acquire links to 100s of pages advising you on how not to procrastinate while writing your novel or thesis, following a fitness program, or seeking a new career. These are all challenging endeavors, and individuals who follow them ought to be admired even if they do procrastinate.

All procrastinators, regardless how baffled, may boast at least one accomplishment: they haven't quit on their dream. If they had, they wouldn't be concerned about procrastinating on it.

To hang onto a challenging dream despite one's fears, and likewise (frequently) despite disheartenment and disapproval from those around us and society itself, requires vision, dedication and bravery. So, rather than seeing your procrastination issue as a shameful defect, attempt viewing it instead as a symbol of something enceinte inside you.

Yeah, you've got a little work to do to recognize your full potential like who hasn't. But at least you continue showing up and fighting the great fight.

A different reason not to feel bad about your procrastination issue is that pretty much everybody procrastinates.

Let's likewise not forget that ambitious dreamers choose to follow exceptionally hard goals otherwise, they'd be ambitionless dreamers, right? Average life is pretty complex stuff, but in addition to the complexities of average life, ambitious dreamers may expect to face financial risk if not likely impoverishment; emotional risk and rejection; lack of support from loved ones and/or society; and nerve-wracking working conditions. And that doesn't even count the underlying difficulties of the goal itself i.e., the need of the person to perfect her craft and sell her work, or to finish a product.

A lot of individuals flee from these sorts of stresses, and I, for one, can't blame them. The issue, however, is that in doing so they likewise flee from their aspirations.

Ruth Walker

Whenever I teach, I remind my pupils who are frequently deeply ashamed of their procrastination issue of the many individuals who have given up on their aspirations.

We all share a minute of sadness for those individuals, and then I softly congratulate my pupils for persevering in their own aspirations despite all the difficulties and barriers.

CHAPTER 4- WHAT'S KEEPING YOU FROM BEING PRODUCTIVE?

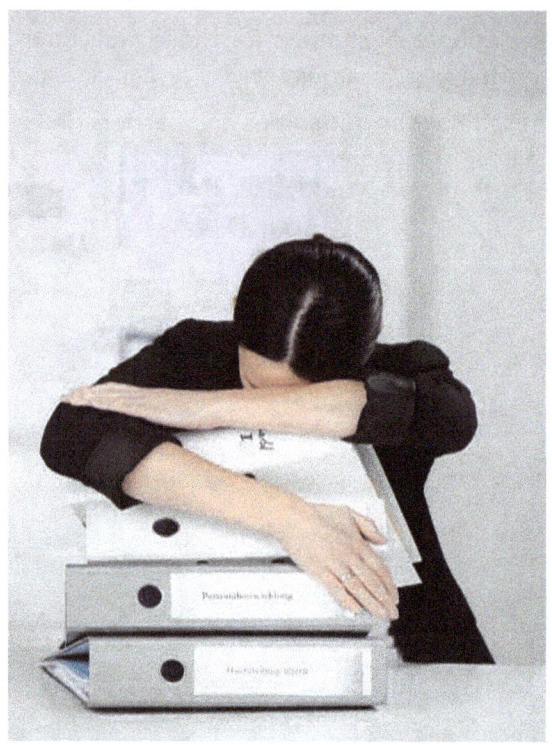

If you're like a lot of people, that question has haunted you for a long time. Among the most frustrating things about procrastination is that it appears like it would be the simplest issue in the world to resolve. Actually, it's among the hardest. Really, that's not quite true. Any issue is difficult to solve, if you're not truly solving it.

I mean it: the only way to resolve an issue is to resolve it. If you attempt to resolve an issue utilizing actions designed to resolve some other issue, or actions designed to resolve no issue at all, but rather to maintain the status quo, then you're bound to bomb. You may try from here to the moon, reining in all the mental capacity, creativity and passion you may muster, and you'll still never resolve the issue.

You likely believe the root issue causing your procrastination is laziness, lack of discipline, lack of self-control, immaturity, lack of commitment, or some similar character defect. But guess what? It's probably none of those.

Firstly, most procrastinators are not I repeat, not lazy, undisciplined, etc. As a matter of fact, most tend to be dynamos in areas other than the one they're procrastinating in. Among the peculiar agonies of procrastination is that we're frequently productive in areas of our lives other than the one closest to our heart.

Secondly applying damaging labels like "lazy" or "undisciplined" to yourself is, from a problem-solving standpoint, worse than worthless. Not only do those labels misidentify the issue, they really make the situation worse by sabotaging your self-assurance and predisposing you to failure.

Moreover, people frequently live up or down to the labels; so that if somebody repeatedly calls you, or you repeatedly call yourself, lazy or uncommitted, you're likely to live "down" to that label.

More often than not, solving, or resolving, an issue is a rather trivial exercise when we understand what the problem is. Treating procrastination as a symptom of laziness or a lack of discipline doesn't work, as those are not the causes of procrastination. Instead, they're symptoms, just like procrastination itself is a symptom, of a deeper issue. That issue is commonly either:

You were never taught the habits of productive work. As we live in a vacuum, this likely means you've rather learned the "default" habits of low productivity or non-productivity.

These results in what I call Behavior Based Procrastination.

Or,

Fear: of change, success, failure, etc.

This results in what I call Dread Based Procrastination.

Frequently, individuals suffer from both.

Behavior Based Procrastination is a comparatively easy issue to define and solve.

Dread Based Procrastination is more complex. Unlike Behavior Based Procrastination, which is commonly caused by a lack of data or training, dread Based Procrastination is caused by, as its name implies, concern.

Dread is unfortunately a major force in a lot of people's lives: it's frequently a rational, if not optimal, reaction to the troubles and stresses of life and an ambitious path.

Have a look at the ways you can prevent disasters from happening.

• Produce schemes that work

Create schemes that would allow you to better use your time by encouraging the free flow of work. Systematize and organize stuff so that there's a procedure that leads one step to work with the next step and so forth and so on. Don't begin over every time you have to produce something.

• Produce schemes to address repetitive jobs

This would include any paper and/or digital technology that you'd utilize to get the job done in your business. Forever have enough supplies available that you are able to readily get at.

Utilize a calendar, digital or paper, to keep track of appointments. You are able to see what, wear and when you have to do what every day, at-a-glance. This may help you successfully plan your day for optimum results.

Forever work with a clean desk, with papers filed and organized and forever have the most frequently utilized items for your business in your immediate grasp.

• Plan enough rest periods

Sleep authorities recommend for the normal, healthy grownup to get at least eight hours of sleep a night. This helps them to function decently and be really productive, yet a poll by the National Sleep Foundation's 2000 Sleep in America omnibus poll discovered that, on the average, grownups sleep just under seven hours during the work week.

As an enterpriser, you ought to schedule a sufficient amount of rest for optimal productivity. The amount is different for each of us and you ought to let your body see what circumstances it works best under.

Some require 8 hours, some more, others less. Your body recognizes the answer.

• Formulate your communication skills

Your ability to aptly and confidently communicate what you understand both orally and in writing is extremely crucial to your business' success. Make it an in progress commitment to continue to better your speaking and writing skills. You'll save time and have a more successful vocation.

What Happens If You're Not Organized?

Simple tasks like setting goals, making lists, creating processes that optimize productivity is almost a chore as the individual's disorganized state will effectively cause the overwhelming feeling of being totally lost.

When this happens the likelihood of giving up any endeavor before it is completed becomes a norm thus contributing to a very negative habit to indulge in. This will eventually have a direct impact on other people too, as the individual cannot be considered dependable thus effecting the relationships on many different levels.

Therefore it would be prudent for the individual to take a step back and seriously consider how the lack of being organized is affecting the various aspects of his or her life and that of those around.

Being disorganized may have many different connotation linked to it and finding out which ones are contributing to this negative behaviors can sometimes help to eradicate or at the very least control the urge to be disorganized.

People who are frustrated with their lives are often the one who are also very much disorganized. Linking both these factors together has been proven to produce the expected results of negativity.

Not having the moral commitment which simply equates disrespect for others, their time and their commitments is another prevalent issue behind not wanting to be more organized in one's own undertakings.

Generally people who are selfish fail to develop this moral commitment trait and continue to assume everyone will be accommodating and forgiving of their follies.

CHAPTER 5- HOW TO BE MORE PRODUCTIVE?

The following are some tips to follow in the quest to overhaul the property and yet bust the bank:

In action #1, the word "exactly" means precisely. 8:00 a.m., not 8:01, 8:05, or even 8:10. You have to train yourself to be precisely where you're supposed to be not thinking of it, not on the way, not pouring a cup of coffee at the precise moment you're supposed to be there.

In action #2, the word "directly" means that, about a minute after your butt hits the chair, you start your work. "The work you're supposed to be doing" ought to be self-explanatory by now, but let's be extra heedful and remind ourselves that ad lib unscheduled calls (even "urgent" ones), coffee sipping, paper reading, net surfing, and additional activities are all procrastination, pure and simple.

So is doing other work even crucial, good feeling work that wasn't scheduled for this period. You may spend your complete life immersed in these activities, and make little or no progress on your most crucial goals.

In action #3, the word "centered" means that you're flirting with your task, and only your task. Put differently, you're not thinking of other work you may be doing, or your worries regarding your task, or philosophical issues related to your task. And, naturally, you're not thinking of your personal life, last night's TV program, or the birds cheeping enticingly outside your window.

"20 minutes or more." The amount of time one may, or should, remain centered on work differs from person to person. Most individuals, however, may train themselves to work in a centered manner for at least 20 minutes before having to get up and take a break.

After your break and your breaks ought to be as long as you need them to be, particularly when you're 1st tackling your procrastination issue you may return to work for another 20 minutes.

At first, however, working for 20 minutes might seem as unrealistic as flying to the moon. So begin with 10 minutes, or 5, or 2 if you have to. Then, take as long a break as you require, praise yourself for your accomplishment, and repeat.

As you become more and more comfortable with your work, you may build up to 10 minutes of sustained work, then 15, 20, 30, etc. The key is to be patient and not push it.

Habits of a Productive Businessman

• Preparation

Take time to set aside at least 10 minutes every evening to schedule the following day. You ought to normally schedule about 60-70% of your time to allow for disruptions and emergencies. Draw from your list of things that are high priority and arrange blocks of time where you work at a particular area of your business.

• Organize

Take the time to organize your office by class. Do this by putting all of your pertinent files and info that corresponds together in one place. Put all of your financial paperwork together. Put all of your financial-related matters together. This will help you center on one project at a time and be a welcomed time-saver. Orchestrate your office in addition to orchestrating your time. Utilization lists to keep yourself centered and on track. Being organized is a continual procedure. Spending a couple of hours organizing yourself now will save you 100s of hours in the time to come.

• File Systems

A great filing and paperwork system will let you be highly productive. Set your files to reflect the following things:

• To accomplish

Naturally, this would hold everything that you aim to accomplish or have accomplished on a periodic basis, whether that's every day, every week, every quarter or every month. Succinct to accomplish lists are vital to the success of the home business person. You ought to and may likewise file away any old to accomplish lists after having finished them. This will give you archived data and referencing in case you have to go back and seek client or project info.

• To study

There is not adequate time in the entrepreneur's day to study all of the e-mails, postal mail material, magazines, e-books and catalogs that come across his desk or PC. When you've information that's coming from a lot of sources both online and offline, you have to be certain to keep them organized for future reference. File away this material for future reviewing and studying when more time is permissible.

Keep a tickler file online and offline so that you are able to easily access them both at will. Particularly in cases of net filing, you are able to do several matters to better manage your time.

1.) Sort your mail into a digital folder with a label to make it future access easier.

2.) Upload it to your e-mail inbox or e-mail provider.

3.) Transfer the folder to your PDA or additional technological devices

4.) Later or if time permits, view the correspondence and either a.) Erase it or b.) To act on it

• Thoughts

Utilize the thoughts folder to hold your originative thoughts and any future thoughts you have for the business. This may likewise be a part of your goals and goal setting, but ought to definitely hold creative thinking thoughts and sparks. You are able to likewise utilize this folder to hold additional ideas or marketing strategies that you chance upon. This is to set the stage to spark more thoughts inside you when you review the folder. This folder has the potential to grow significantly as a big part of any home business is promoting, promoting, promoting.

• Resolutions

This folder will bear resolutions to either correspondence that you've sent to likely or present customers or answers that you're providing for yourself. Don't know how much you charged for that final project you did for X Customer? Look in the resolutions folder. What about the quote that you gave the net phone directory company after they asked about your telecommerce services...it may very well be in the resolutions folder. Resolutions may be in response to questions that you've sent out or have received into your office.

• References

The reference folder is vital to your business and helps enormously with marketing efforts. You ought to have correspondence that is referrals for preceding jobs and letters of recommendations in that folder. The reference folder ought to (and may) likewise hold references that you require for other types of projects where another individual is needed. Put differently, if you are a content author but have to find a web designer, look in your reference folder and see who recommends whom as that. This may be a priceless piece of time management and organizational tool for your business. Maximize its utilization by notating and documenting pertinent and relevant info that's highly targeted to particular niche areas.

• Copies

Everything that happens upon your desk ought to be copied in some manner. That includes purchase receipts, contracts, bills, tax info, client work orders and any and everything that pertains to your business. In order to lessen the amount of clutter that this may cause, digitally copy everything and store it on your PC or on a back-up disk. Very simply, scan documents into your PC and save it to a specified area. This makes it much simpler to recall it when you require it.

• File

Pretty self-explanatory, this tickler file is for everything that has to be filed away. Develop a scheme that's simple to remember and takes the guessing out of "where may it be?" This system will let you find the info that you want when you want it, keeping it out of your way and off of your desk.

• PC

Learn to utilize your computer effectively and efficiently. Discover ways to take full advantage of it and maximize its utilization for your business. Invest in courses or at least buy how-to books for every program in your system. Your PC may make your days more productive and streamlined toward effective time management if it's properly utilized. Learning it in its totality and the numerous features that it has will help you make better utilization of your time.

• Creative thinking

Creative thinking is the spark and backbone of any successful net business. Without it, ideas can't take form and businesses can't be formed. A mind that's relaxed, stress-free and happy is more conducive to sparks and bouts of creative thinking and has more time to center fully on attaining good business. Spend originative time thinking, reading and exploring ways and thoughts that may improve your business. Little bits of time on a day-to-day basis may help and result in effective techniques.

• Delineating projects

Making an outline of projects will help the work at home person make more beneficial use of their days and maximize utilization of their time. In order to see a more generative day, it's great to begin with an outline and work from it. Firstly, list where you want the end result of the project to be. From there, work backward and formulate the steps that it will take to get there. After that, conclude the outline with the opening move of the project and the brainstorming idea(s) that were used to spark the project from the outset. Once you work this way, you're basically reducing big projects to smaller, manageable sorts to see results. Work slower, more methodically and cautiously to avoid making errors.

• Plan around disruptions

Disruptions tend to happen in identifiable patterns with most of them occurring early in the day versus later in the day. Disruptions are never handy nor do they "choose" a time to occur. Plan to do bigger projects for later in the day or later in the week when there tends to be fewer disruptions.

• Allot deadlines

Deadlines move individuals to action and acquire quick results. Without deadlines, matters simply get accomplished when they get accomplished with no haste behind them. Make a deadline and you'll be moved to action.

Chapter 6- Of Employees, Coworkers and Supplies

You may have heard the old saying that a good workman always takes care of his tools. This is equally relevant, whether you work in an office, on a jobsite, or from home. Keeping all of your supplies in excellent working order and easily accessible will make you more productive.

No matter what kinds of supplies you use during your average work day, neglect can slow you down. You cannot do a job effectively if your supplies are broken, damaged, or worn out from use. If you try to use supplies which are not in good condition, the quality of your work can suffer. It can take you much longer to get things done, and they will not be done as well as they would with supplies that are in top-notch condition.

Think of it this way: if you are trying to work on a computer that is not up to par, or using a hand tool that is bent or otherwise damaged, or a piece of office equipment which stalls while you are operating it, your productivity can come to a complete standstill.

You may become frustrated or angry, and possibly not get the job done at all. When all of your supplies, tools, and equipment are kept in ideal condition, they are in better shape to do the job properly. Your work will not be slowed down, and you will not risk errors from faulty equipment.

Good supplies in good condition mean getting things done and having the best results. No matter how much of a hurry you are in to complete a task and end a work day, taking a few minutes to be sure everything is in good shape will save you time and eliminate unnecessary frustration. You can also make a point of replacing damaged supplies or equipment as soon as possible. You can take this positive new habit even further by making sure all of your supplies and equipment are put away.

These new habits will benefit you, as well as everyone else who uses the same supplies and equipment. When everything is checked for good condition and put away, they will all be in good condition and easily accessible the next time you or someone else needs them. It will make your work day proceed that much smoother, and you will be more productive.

Is Creating an Environment of Competition The Best Way to Boost Productivity?

There is a trend that is popular in the business world today. Some people believe that competition is the best way to boost productivity. No matter what line of work you are in, it is very likely that this approach will backfire.

First, teamwork is much better than competition. When you use the approach that everyone is working for the common good of the company, more will get done. When the sense of competition is eliminated, each person will want to contribute his very best simply because it is his place to do so. He will not feel that he must outdo his coworkers, which in turn will increase the feeling of teamwork. When everyone is working as a team, and working toward a common goal, productivity will increase.

Second, everyone needs to feel that he is valued. This is as true in the workplace as anywhere else. The best employee, and the employee who gets more done, is the one who believes that his work is appreciated. Another factor in increasing productivity is to reduce the amount of tension, friction, and conflict in the workplace. When there are employees who make a point of not getting along with others, expecting someone else to do their jobs for them, or simply being difficult to be around on a regular basis, these kinds of problems should be dealt with as quickly as possible.

All it takes is one or two people who like to argue, or shirk their responsibilities onto others, to turn any workplace into an uncomfortable place where no one can concentrate on doing their jobs. It is important to eliminate these problems so that everyone in the workplace can get things done.

Productivity is at its best in the workplace where everyone present gets along. This does not mean wasting time with unnecessary chatting and visiting. Simply acknowledging that everyone is there for the same purpose is usually enough. The workplace should be a place where every employee feels comfortable. It should be a place where everyone knows that his coworkers all have the same goals in mind.

When each person knows that he is a valuable part of the company, and a valuable part of the team, each person will feel more confident and will be more productive.

Ruth Walker
Reward Yourself From Time to Time

Encouraging yourself by rewarding yourself along the line can be a good thing. Unfortunately, if it is approached the wrong way it can be more trouble than it is worth. If you believe you owe yourself time off, special treats or something else noteworthy every time you accomplish something, you will soon find yourself accomplishing very little. Instead of seeing it as a reward for a job well done, you may start to feel as if you are entitled to rewards or special favors for completing tasks which are within your scope of responsibility anyway. This is why granting yourself little "extras" for doing your job is not usually a good idea.

It is even more negative if you expect special recognition or rewards from your boss or coworkers for doing what you are supposed to do. Rewarding yourself along the line as if you have made a spectacular accomplishment is not the best way to go about getting the job done. Instead, applying some self-encouragement should be the only reward you need. When you complete a task on time, or do a project especially well, you can acknowledge it as a small but important success.

When you apply this kind of self-encouragement with a figurative pat on the back, you are rewarding yourself for a job well done. You will also be prepared to move on to the next task or the next step. This concept works equally well whether you work on your own or in a group. If no one feels compelled to believe that he should gain some kind of special recognition for doing his job, getting the job done will be the priority.

In work settings which include a number of people working together as a group, no one will feel more or less important than anyone else. Each person will realize that he is expected to contribute something, without expecting to receive anything

Habits of a Productive Businessman

unique for doing it. Encouraging yourself along the way will serve to keep your spirits up and your sense of motivation at its peak. While significant accomplishments may result in some kind of little extra reward, self-encouragement should be the only reward necessary for doing your job.

ABOUT THE AUTHOR

Ruth Walker was born in Los Angeles as the only daughter of Atty. Jason Walker and Dr. Angela Walker. From a well-off family, Ruth lived the good life until the untimely demise of her parents in a car crash.

Following the death of her parents, Ruth was left to manage the family estate. Before she was in college, she was already familiar of the many things needed to keep her wealth growing. That is why; it was only practical that she chose to study business and finance in Princeton.

Today, Ruth has built an empire. She continues to inspire other people through her various charity works and pro bono consultations.

www.ingramcontent.com/pod-product-compliance
Lightning Source LLC
Chambersburg PA
CBHW051252170526
45165CB00004B/1678